GROWING UP IN AFRICA

A Short Story of
Self Discovery
in an
Age of Innocence

RORY JOHNSTON

Copyright © 2012 Rory Johnston
All rights reserved.
ISBN: 1478311398
ISBN 13: 9781478311393

This short story is dedicated to Virginia Ann who opened my eyes to love and life.

THE BEGINNING

I don't remember much and I have gathered most of what happened in my formative years from snatches of memory of oft-repeated stories told to me by my parents. It was the end of World War II, and my father had returned from service in the British Army. He had come back to Edinburgh, Scotland, to finish his medical studies. Residency, I believe it is called—his medical career had been interrupted by the war. Realizing the very bleak economic future that post-war Britain offered a young doctor, my parents, with my two young brothers in tow, decided to head to South Africa!

It was a land of great promise back then (before the insane racial purity ideas took hold), and my grandmother's family had immigrated to the Eastern Cape in the 1820s. They had prospered and had several sheep farms of note. My father was about to become a sheep farmer. As far as I know, all he knew about sheep came as a genetic memory from our ancestors who lived on the Scottish Borders and would frequently raid the English down south and relieve them of their flocks and maidens! Anyway, sheep farming was the plan. I think that secretly, without ever admitting it, my father was envisaging the close proximity of the African big-game-hunting fields and being able to indulge his passion—screw the sheep farming. So it was onto the Mail Boat for the two-week cruise to East London.

Somewhere along the way I arrived at the Mater Dei Hospital in East London. I hope the good sisters forgive my current feelings for their church, and I am pleased that they gave me a trouble-free arrival—for the start at least. I don't have much on the first few years other than that I was somewhat disparagingly referred to by the very busty and formidable Xhosa nurses as "a little pink thing." Was that me in entirety—or were they referring to a particular part of my anatomy? This became a source of constant anxiety to me ever since and a story my mother thought hilarious. She never ceased to tell to anyone who would listen. Gee, thanks Mom.

Then came the newspaper advertisement for a doctor to establish a medical corps for the Rhodesian Army and Air Force—Southern Rhodesia was a self-governing country under the oversight of the British Government at that time. The long and the short was that my dad got the job—after all, he was an accomplished and highly decorated war vet and a medical doctor, and he was eager to get closer to the big game (his secret)! There was a rail journey I believe; must have been hell—the route went up through the Transvaal and then into the desert of Bechuanaland. Imagine my poor mother from the Highlands of Scotland coping with the stifling, pre-air-conditioning heat, three boys, and thorn scrub for miles and miles of Bloody Africa. She had a totally different vision, slightly less romantic, to that of Hemingway.

That was, anyhow, how I arrived at the airbase and maybe started to think for myself.

EARLY IMPRESSIONS OF AFRICA

I had all manner of jumbled thoughts before I could remember where I was or what I was doing. Out of the fog of memory came our house in Hatfield, Rhodesia, Africa. My parents were so proud and hardworking, and were able to replicate an English bungalow in the heart of the African bush—replete with a granite fireplace reminiscent of the Tudor times. It even had a low rock wall on the front—no doubt to repel the invading hordes, which sure looked good and kept those poor penniless work seekers out of our front yard.

A mere fifty feet away across the road was the virgin African bush, protected by our wise city fathers as a greenbelt—if only we had been as perceptive as they were sixty years ago! This was my hideout—sitting in the center of the savannah was a huge granite boulder, spewed from some volcanic cataclysm centuries ago and ending arse-upwards in the middle of my backyard. This was my playground from day one—climbing up the fissure in the middle of the backside, escaping the slime from the other folks claiming right of ownership to my rock (hyrax—relatives of the elephant, they say). The Rock was where I was to discover life as I progressed through it and I spoke to it as one would speak to God.

Snatches of my life before knowing my own personal Rock of Gibraltar come thru the distant fog. I remember being able to climb into my parent's bed and experience, to me, the indescribable bliss of warmth and closeness. Mind you, after reaching about four years old, that was all I was to get in that department. It was a hug-free zone growing up in Africa—wasn't done, old chap. If I think about it, I have been playing catch-up all these years and will probably never get over that particular form of sensory deprivation. I apologize here and now to the poor folks who have looked to me for love.

Running over a seemingly benign white-ash barbeque pit from the previous night with my bare feet in the morning! No one told me about the longevity of African hardwood embers. The young Shona lad assigned to guard me laughed and chattered incomprehensibly—I think the gist of what he was saying was that never having had shoes, his feet were so iron-clad, and that only a soft whitey like me would have been burnt! Not sure he lasted in our employ too long—the bliss of an immature memory.

We were living pre-Rock then on the edge of an airbase, and I can still see the lumbering DC-3s taking to the air just across the driveway—today the sound of the Pratt and Whitney engines are so firmly imprinted in my mind that I can hear a good old Dak, as that aircraft is still fondly called, from miles away. Our neighbor was in charge of keeping those birds in the air, and one beautiful African morning he stopped by to chat. He was talking to my mother through the living room window. I heard a "knock, knock" at the glass-fronted door and, "Canada Dry" ginger ale in hand, I went to open it. Not being very tall at the time, imagine my horror to be confronted with a huge, fully hooded, and extremely angry venomous Egyptian Cobra in the process of attacking its opposition, reflected in the mirror of the glass! Thank goodness self-preservation kicked in as I hurled the bottle of soda at cobra number one and I slammed the door. I ran into the living room wailing and jumped onto the sofa, blubbering as only a five-year-old can do. The poor snake, only doing what snakes do after all, was unfortunately dispatched by our neighbor with a blast of a mere 12 gauge. I, since then, on the other hand, have an intense dislike for our wriggly friends to this day.

Then we moved—what bliss I thought, I had my own room! My brothers were sent off in the colonial manner to boarding school. Yea Gods—if I think my life is screwed up, I hate to think how they made it through. It is a quaint English institution, the boarding school. Make a man of you, son! Backbone! Anyway—they were off and I was left to my parents, who did their best, I suppose. But in reality I was an irritation. Funds did not permit me to be sent off the boarding school at that level so I was entrusted to the local public school, two and one half miles away by bicycle. And wouldn't you believe it—downhill! So here I was speeding down the hill to school…just what started my rebellion. I was faced every day with the tedious climb back up the hill to return to loneliness and emptiness. This is when the Rock came into play!

THE ROCK

Can you imagine in your mind's eye a flat plain of golden grass that makes up much of the African savannah? The wind stirs and rustles the dry stalks as the relentless heat bears down, day after day. It harbors a myriad of creatures, big and small, waiting for those first drops of rain to turn on the faucet in a desperate frenzy of life and reproduction. For the most part, the high plateau of Rhodesia where I grew up was like that—nine months of dry and three months of renewal and frantic replication of self.

My Rock, as you know, was out there in the midst of the surrounding savannah. It waited for me and my almost daily pilgrimage. I knew all the Rock's hand holds to hoist me up the crevice—I could have done it blindfolded. Up to the top and security—actually no, the inner altar was a little off to the side, a six-by-three hole somehow hollowed out of the dense granite—perfect for me to burrow into. How it got there I have no idea, but years later, learning about igneous rocks, I realize that it would have been a gentle burp on the side of that huge semi-molten rock as it cooled after being hurled from the bowels of the earth. The burp became my altar where I would scurry in and contemplate what life had served me up and how I was to deal with it.

There I was, a timid, thin, and callow youth in my sanctum sanctorum. Here I could develop a survival strategy! It was where I could dream about what existed elsewhere and even think, God forbid, about having friends to play with. No children of my age lived anywhere near me so having a yearning for buddies was a strange concept, but very true, in those lonely days. Anyway—more than anything, it gave me peace and strength to see nature as the Creator expected it to be. Back at home I was being trained in two very different universes. Dad, you see, was the big-game-hunter army guy, and naturally I was expected to be adept at the rifle. I loved at that early age to handle the air guns, and my pride of joy was a .22-caliber single shot. It was not what rifles could do that fascinated me but the fact that I could aim the shots in a very tight circle. The kill was not my objective. I did it, however, and it secretly filled me with horror. I asked the Rock the wisdom of this and was given the vision that I was looking at a very finite world and to be careful. Years later I realized the futility of killing and looked back to the Rock and asked myself—why did it take me so long to open my eyes?

It was my fantasyland too! How many kids have their very own huge Rock to claim as their own? I would be defending my feudal kingdom at one stage, repelling all attacks from the dastardly swine trying to trick me coming up the hidden flank. Then it could be the huge aircraft carrier that I was silently maneuvering into position without betraying myself to the unsuspecting enemy flotilla in the grasslands below.

Yet it was always the refuge. Daily I was faced with nothingness when I reached home from school. I would walk away from that dismal scenario and hop over the granite wall, over the road, and up the path to the tranquility, escapism, and sanity of my Rock. It was where I was able confront, but maybe not conquer, my fears.

MASTALA BAMUSI—A SON OF LAKE NIASSA

Lake Niassa is a huge Central African freshwater lake in the Great Rift Valley, situated in the present-day state of Malawi. Blessed with few natural resources, Malawi has traditionally relied on the remit of its peoples who ventured out into Africa with nothing else to offer than their labor and hard work. This is still happening to this day, as it was sixty odd years ago.

Into the Rock era came one Mastala Bamusi as our "house boy"—in those days this was chief chef, house cleaner, and general aide to my father as the dispenser of highly starched military uniforms. As for my mother, he was also chief ignorer of her commands and thus a constant source of irritation for her!

Always one for protocol, Mastala would begin his day at breakfast and enter the dining room. He was always very formally attired in his colonially correct white, starched uniform and superb bright red fez headgear—complete with black tassel. No Shriner here—but a superbly proud son of Africa! No shoes of course…The usual courtesies were exchanged— "Good morning, Master," to which my father would reply, "Good Morning, Masta." How my parents did not see the supreme irony of this interchange

I do not know, but it sent me into silent mirth. No address to my mother of course—a mere woman. Must have pissed her off no end.

Just to rub in her irrelevance to him, Masta would have a placemat ritual at the dining room table. We had a set of animal-print placemats of various species. Without fail my father would get the elephant—naturally, as the head of the African household. I got the graceful kudu antelope with beautiful spiral horns and my brothers various other inoffensive species. Unfailingly my mother got the giraffe—her long neck peering into affairs he did not deem worthy, surprisingly finding dusty areas, and generally poking her nose where it should not be!

With me having no other friends and little guidance from my parents, Mastala, or Masta as I would prefer, became a confidante for me—sharing his hard-earned wisdom and offering me guidance as far as he could, given the strict boundary of those colonial times. I remember even sharing his *sadza* (ground cornmeal) cookies he would make on a flat iron plate for me as a special treat. He knew about the Rock—he would follow the bush path towards it once a week but continue on down into the valley below. It was a Sunday ritual. There lay the small grass-hut village that had the brew and the drums that gave him the weekly escape from the rigid life which enabled him to send those funds to the family back in the highlands of the Great Rift Valley.

He knew about me—maybe more than any other person really, as he had a blank check. No one else was looking, and he was my only real counsel, my only real listener. You can imagine my delight when my mother's Bantam roosters, named somewhat unexplainably Banda and Chipembere (Niassa political rivals at that time) had the predestined fight of dominance in which the young Chipembere triumphed over miserable Banda. You see, Chipembere was Masta's tribal leader and thus naturally my hero—we had talked at length together about the injustice wrought over the land of his birth by Dictator President Banda, and this indeed was justice!

Masta traveled with us on our safaris into the remotest areas of the country—with his uncanny ability to establish a working bush kitchen from

A Short Story of Self Discovery in an Age of Innocence

a patch of grass within a few hours. He enjoyed those journeys as a break from the dreary monotony imposed by my mother's weekly unchanging menu and cleaning demands. It was a chance to be mano a mano (as close as one could get in those days, given the racial divide) with the hunting men, together with the promise of all that free protein. One early morning at our camp on the banks of the Umniati River in winter after a freezing-cold night (yes it can get below zero sometimes in Africa!), we were all lying in our camp beds struggling to keep warm and waiting beyond the normal rise of the weak sun to send some heat our way. Into the picture came Masta, scurrying around and readying the kettle for coffee, picking up the water can, evidently heavy, then attempting to pour into the kettle—nothing? The look of astonishment on his face was priceless—poor equatorial Masta had his first experience of frozen water! After getting over his indignation at the howls of mirth around the camp, he in turn collapsed with belly laughs of pure innocent joy.

Masta would return to his homeland once a year ostensibly to plant and harvest his annual corn crop. Year after year the time spent away would grow, and we would have to endure a miserable series of temporary charlatans with dubious resumes. After years of receiving the inevitable call from the embassy that Masta needed another return ticket my parents finally worked it out! Masta would sell the prepaid return portion and gamble that my parents would have reached such a level of desperation in his absence they would fork out another payment. They gave up and I was devastated. Of course, to admit to anyone a friendship across the color line was not done in those days—but that old man from Niassa sure was the only buddy I had then, and I thank him eternally for his wisdom and tolerance of an awkward youth.

EARLY ROCK DAYS

The move from the airbase to Hatfield and the Rock was premeditated by my parents. Dad worked at Army HQ all across town miles away, which would have been the natural choice to settle. But they decided on a very ordinary suburb closest to the airbase because Dad knew he had three sons to educate and would need more funds than his service salary would provide. The Air Force needed a qualified medic every time they practiced night flying, and by taking himself off at night to watch over the flying-crew safety, he made the sacrifice to provide for his children with the overtime pay. Mother would take off during the day to look after pre- and post-natal mothers and the good works of the Woman's Institute. Both had their agendas to help the family, and I was left to fend for myself.

The house was surrounded by about an acre of land and fronted by the famous low granite wall—remember, to repel the hordes? Dotting the garden and shading the lovely grass lawn coaxed out of the dry, sandy soil were several lovely Msasa trees, unique to the land, and who bore witness through their lovely turning leaves to the passing of the seasons. Pride of place in the far corner was the huge Kaffir-Boom tree (otherwise known as the common coral or by its Latin name Erythrina lysistemon) that I loved for its bright red flowers and red seeds delivered in twins in hard pods. They were called lucky beans and were highly collectable by youngsters hoping for their dreams to come true! African Lotto! Not only did I love it, but so did two African Hoopoes (Upupa epops africana), lovely crested birds who came every year just prior to the rains to use their long beaks to prise off the bark to get the awakening bugs beneath. Such is the cycle of nature.

Across the road that bore the path to the Rock was the dry grassland. It was home to dust devils and wrigglys—but I got to know it well. It held a wealth of life that survived in such a hostile environment. Occasionally we would witness the inhabitants of this sere world venture into the lushness of our artificial garden. A pair of hesitant steenbok with their quivering, ever-alert steps would jump over the wall! These beautiful, tiny antelope mate for life. Where the hell did I go wrong? I would watch them, not moving for fear of them taking flight, and take such delight in their moist eyes and twitching noses as they could not resist the lure of that green, greedy gorge about to come! I wonder how they survived in the long winter months, and I was glad we offered a helping hand with that greenery.

The early days were punctuated by boring monotony for me—aged six or seven I guess, cycling back and forth to school. In today's world I would make a claim for child abuse! Especially on the uphill ride back home! School was of no interest to me in those days. I preferred to be in my own private world watching my tiny antelope or walking out to my Rock to commune with it—I had no one else to talk to except poor Masta.

From time to time, exciting things happened! Christmas Day! Both lounge and dining room were draped in faded paper decorations, resurrected year by year. This was to get us into a spiritual frame of mind I am sure! Masta, dutifully adorned at such a momentous occasion with red fez and tassel, would bring in with much fanfare the prize roast turkey. Parents and friends suitably lit up with copious amounts of Pimms No. 1 (another English import of lethal, but gorgeous, liquor), we would celebrate the traditional English Christmas dinner in the unlikely 100-degree African summer. All innocent fun, really.

A Short Story of Self Discovery in an Age of Innocence

One Christmas Day was completely opposite. Sitting down to celebrate the coming feast, we heard a distant "thump," and rushing out the door we saw the awful, billowing, dark-black cloud rising up into the air over at the airbase…Dad knew immediately and leapt, with mother in tow, into the Land Rover and headed off to the almost-certain scene of destruction. They came back hours later, desolate and depressed. A French airliner carrying refugees from the political upheaval in the nearby Belgian Congo had crashed on take off—the quantities of noxious fuel had done the worst on the poor survivors. Mother's prize Christmas present of luxury lipstick was used up to identify the burn victims as they went into the triage, a use the makers "En France" would have never understood. A huge gloom settled over the house. My parents set off to shower and found our lovable black lab soundly asleep on their bed—he had discovered the Cadbury's "Black Magic" box of chocolates, which was a present to my mother and of immense value in darkest Africa in those days, and he had helped himself. The poor chap had such a sugar rush he was not able to paw off the brown paper wrappers from his mouth! Everyone was called in to witness our loss and his snoring pleasure—the spell was broken and we were able to laugh in the awful presence of such tragedy.

High days and holidays apart, I had a slow life. No nearby friends to play with, brothers off at boarding school, and for the most part no parents of the hugging variety. It was the start of my retreat into myself and the trust of only myself. After all, I could talk to myself without fear of contradiction! The answers to my questions came from the Rock and all that surrounded it—the grasses, the trees, the rotation of the seasons—I became a believer of nature—no manmade church or cathedral for me. I drew my strength and self-reliance from the nature that surrounded me. I could talk to it, look at it, cherish and protect it—it became far more reliable to me than the human body politic.

THE FIRST SAFARI

Soon after the move to the Rock, I remember the first safari—a Swahili word *Zarafa* meaning a journey or undertaking, entailing a degree of danger. For us it was the "grand adventure!"

Dad had a list—the shovel, tents, tables, complete dishware, and of course his unique patented wooden throne. Throne, you ask? Yes—this was the wooden structure that had pride of place on arrival in camp—it straddled a hastily dug pit, surrounded by a dry-grass fence, and here we had the most modern of all conveniences in the middle of remotest Africa—a loo with a seat! One's life is a series of priorities, but you could not second-guess my dad—he knew what counted!

Anyway, the list translated to packing the Land Rover—we had a few of them over the years. A Mark One was the first—a marvel of British engineering, but they did get you thru in the end. Who but the British would perfect a vehicle that had the gas tanks underneath the seats? Indeed, to fill up, you would open the passenger-side door, rip aside the seat, open up, and voilà! Let's sit on forty gallons of highly combustible fuel in 120-degree heat! Bloody marvelous! Years later at sixteen years old, I drove a Mark

One for a six-hundred-mile journey—my only indicator of fuel left was a twelve-inch ruler as a primitive dipstick. I guess that ability of stating and ignoring the obvious was why the British were able to paint the map of Africa bright red.

Once stocked and stacked, we would set off to a place unknown. Towards the Zambezi Valley. In those days it was a hazardous place and was reached only by miles upon miles of "strip" roads. A social welfare engineering project at the end of World War II opened up the country with twin twelve-inch ribbons of tar designed to accommodate the axel width of most vehicles. British, you were OK—American? Tough buddy—you got to drag one wheel. The interesting part of strip roads was the incoming vehicle-approach tactic—courtesy dictated a move to the shoulder with one wheel riding on the tar. The brave or foolish hoped to stay on all two! "Chicken!"

The Zambezi was reached by way of Victoria Falls—at that time a sleepy village consisting of the railway siding, the famous Victoria Falls Hotel, a police station, and the Sprayview General Store. There was no road to where we were going. So it was over the magnificent bridge—inspired and built on the empirical design of Cecil Rhodes—how exciting it was! A brief stop was made to see David Livingstone surveying his Mosi-au-Tunya (Smoke That Thunders) and no doubt charging his evangelical batteries from the spray.

Then it was over the span into the slightly second-class "Northern" political partner. To this day I am not sure why my parents regarded and imbued in me that this part of the world was way inferior? After looting African hardwood forests, the Northern side had, however inadvertently, provided the now-disused narrow gauge railway tract as a road to the meeting of the mighty Zambezi and Chobe rivers. We engaged the four-wheel drive, and upstream we went to Kazungula. From there we would cross into Bechuanaland Protectorate (just who were the British protecting, I always wondered?). We crossed over the river via a cattle ferry, hastily converted with timber 2 x 6s to accommodate the Land Rover.

A Short Story of Self Discovery in an Age of Innocence

Then we were on our own—heading back on the more developed "Southern" partner—you kidding? Zero. Following game tracks, pushing aside trees—I shudder to think of the wholesale environmental damage we committed—who thought about that in those days? Soon our campsite was reached on the banks of the Zambezi River. This spot on Earth closely rivaled my Rock—a birthplace of discovery, growth, and self-sufficiency. There was an awareness of others less fortunate—locals with no access to what today we consider birthrights: basic health care, schooling, vaccines, you name it. My arrogant bubble was starting to be pierced...The word spread up and down the banks of this mighty river that the doctor had arrived! Soon they would come, as Dad knew, as he was always well equipped with quantities of medicine. He knew what to expect. I did not. Coming face-to-face with youngsters who had walked for miles to see someone with such pale skin made me sit up—the first awareness of a life of privilege.

GLORIOSA SUPERBA

The Flame Lily. As its Latin name Gloriosa Superba so aptly suggests, this so delicate and stunningly beautiful flower rises out of one of the most hostile environments in the world, as if to challenge those who dare question that nature will triumph in the end.

The dry months in Central Africa and my own savannah playground would test all living beings. The rains would falter around March, and the long dry season would commence. Vestiges of green would shrivel, and the tall tender grasses would harden in protection against the coming drought. Water holes would disappear, and those who could adapt would begin their hibernation, waiting for the promise of the future bounty to come. Or so they hoped?

The long winter would then set in—this was not a Siberian event in Africa but was equally traumatic to those who lived in it. We, of course, were able to cheat. How supremely arrogant we were in retrospect. A distant dam would hold back the precious water, and by modern engineering we were able to keep our lawn green throughout those months—we could even prosper alien species such as roses to thrill our senses, as they loved the warmish days and chill nights.

The sun would rise daily and then set about its process of leaching all moisture—day after day—until about September. Then the great tease would commence—a weather roulette sent to try the patience of all living creatures. A slight hint of moisture would encourage the buildup of huge clouds in the afternoon. Anxious necks would peer upwards and wonder if that day would be the one to provide the relief—a break in the heat, dust, and monotony.

Suddenly—all hell would break lose. Violent crackles of lightning and booms of thunder would roll across the land—followed by the huge drops of that lovely precious liquid that would commence the renewal. But would it last into a daily event? Or would it be a false dawn? Just prior to this onset, the dry savannah would not be able to hold back its tinder, and violent strikes of lightning or some form of spontaneous combustion would set off the dreaded veldt fires. Out of nowhere the flames would rear up, devastating all around—I would watch this and wondered, what was happening to my friends out there? The tiny steenboks—where would they find refuge? The flames would reach the road and thankfully peter out on the dusty sand, leaving behind a blackened wasteland and devastation. My Rock—hidden in a sea of golden grass all those winter months—would sit exposed, its silver bulk sitting even more awkwardly as it was surrounded by nakedness, death, and destruction.

Watch the sky and look for the pregnant clouds! All one could do was to wait as the dust devils stirred up and churned the blackened chards into spirals in the air as if beseeching God to put an end to it all. No escape from the heat and the sweat.

The drips would irritate the dust and blackness into little circles—then out of nowhere we would hear a steady drumbeat on the roof of the rain tumbling out of the sky. A release and a signal to all nature that it was a go—a green light! Almost overnight the burnt stubble would be gone, to be replaced with an emerald green grassy regrowth—leaves would sprout

out of branches long given up for dead. Frantic activity would take over the land, as one never knew how long this bounty would last in Africa.

For me, walking back up to the more suitably attired and skirted in green Rock, there would be one sign I can never forget. Out of the sand, lured by the promise of the eternal elixir of water, would rise what I deem the most exotic of all nature's gifts—Gloriosa superba. The Flame Lily. For a few short days and from a tuber buried far enough below the sand to escape winter's devastation, a thin, frail shoot would appear—to be capped with an orange-to-red flower of such delicacy it is hard to imagine that anything quite as beautiful could exist in all the world.

A USUAL DAY

It was a fairly humdrum existence for a preteen. I would be up with the sun and suitably dressed in my khaki uniform and tie—ready to take on the African day all prepped up as the colonial imitator of the English schoolboy. What on Earth were they thinking of by transplanting a way of life so out of sync in the African heat! Anyway, morning breakfast pleasantries were exchanged—and sly glances were exchanged with Masta, as he and I knew the codes. Then Dad would take off and so would I—bicycling down the hill to the dreaded school. A few words from Masta would give me encouragement to make the trip and yearn for the return. Incongruous, to put it mildly—a tall, austere, and stoic African would give a gangly White youth the equivalent of today's high five and the power to get through the day.

Each approaching turn of the wheels would heighten my foreboding—stashing the bike and lining up for class. First order was a quarter pint of milk—the government's answer to those less fortunate, to enable alertness for six hours of intolerable boredom. Grand idea, but the bottles had been delivered at least four hours previously and had been curdling in the slow microwave heat of the tropical sun. Milk to this day holds little appeal for me.

I had no enthusiasm for the classroom. I was sent to the headmaster numerous times for minor acts of rebellion. I even earned thrashings at that early age. It was of course permitted then and found totally acceptable that recalcitrant youths would earn a birching. Another quaint English import! No wonder we Scots stole their sheep.

In a daily repeated relief, the final bell would toll, and there was no delay in my departure! Up the hill and via the shortcuts through the veldt paths I would pant, pedaling as fast as I could to get out of the stultifying oppression of the valley below. Masta would be there on hand to give me the equivalent of today's milk and cookies.

There I was faced with several choices: to do the homework (not); persuade Masta to take a break from his daily chores to talk; or take off towards the Rock. I usually longed for option two, and as we got to know each other more, I so believe that our conversations became a welcome break for both of us. Mother had a very strict routine and a weekly menu regime—which to my knowledge never varied over the years. Sunday was roast day, which would be translated into a curry-and-rice dinner on Wednesday, week after year. Dad never complained that I was aware, and clearly, cuisine was not one of his hot buttons! But can you imagine the boredom of preparing this rote—no wonder Masta would take a break to chat with me from time to time despite knowing he would incur her wrath and accusations of laziness and sloth.

We had many conversations about his life, which was almost incomprehensible to me—why would anyone leave his family for years at a time to live a life of a single man in a strange land, with a language he could not fully understand and an employer who did not or would ever understand his social mores? Despite all these challenges, he always took the time and patience to sit with me and listen to my questions, even with them being framed from my glaringly obvious position of privilege and although I was totally unaware of this. No less, his slow and considered responses to my naivety were a way of guidance, which I was so wanting from my parents. Not that my parents did not offer teaching, but it was remote; Masta, on the other hand, explained in terms a youngster could understand about how to approach life and take on its hurdles as they came. Our relationship was not always easy—if I got out of line in his eyes, there was always a swift reprimand with voluble diatribes of Chinyanja, which was his native tongue. I knew a few words and would get the message of displeasure without any real understanding of what he was saying.

Little by little he was able to transform the savage in me. At one point my parents thought Latin courses were the answer. Latin? The poor tutor would travel for miles to lecture me about talking to tables just as the Roman's had done. Needless to say, I flew into a brick wall. It was then that Masta told me it might be a good idea to listen to the educators—he had told me all he could about the nature and the seasons that existed over the wall and on the way to the Rock. He had reached the limit of his teaching, and the tug of his homeland was becoming stronger than he could resist. It was then that I realized he was on his way—he had done his job, and it was now up to me.

THE SAFARIS

The term "safari," as I have previously noted, stems from the Arabic word *Zarafa*, meaning a journey of much distance and some danger. We were fortunate to have many, and I was blessed with parents who thought nothing of loading up the Land Rover and striking out for up to a month at a time to parts of Africa that had no roads, no electricity—no anything except as nature intended. This was a thrill and privilege few can imitate in their growing days.

The usual destination was the Zambezi valley to "our" campsite just above the Katambora rapids—a series of volcanic fault lines that tumbled the huge turgid mass of water from the Angolan highlands into crushed whiteness—never mind the Victoria Falls; this lot alone put paid to David Livingstone's dreams of navigating this monster of a river, and thank God too. It had left us a part of nature as it was intended. The power of the water coming over the rapids with such force over the years had crushed the volcanic basalt rocks into a white, powdery sand of such fineness that it actually squeaked when walked upon.

Anyway, a mile or so upstream was our camp—tarpaulins were laid out, camp beds assembled, and mosquito nets strung, Masta had the cooking fires blazing (of course, you know the "throne" was already in place), and we were ready for our first night under the stars of the Milky Way. Looking up into the huge panoply above one could sometimes see shooting stars—not supposed to mention it to anyone for fear of bad luck they say, but someone always did, awed by the majesty of the universe displayed above far from human lights. Then we started to see the satellites—Sputnik, I suppose? They rolled ominously overhead—a harbinger of a world so changed we could not even begin to imagine. The task of dousing the gas light was a duty that changed from night to night, and I cannot forget the time when my mother asked, "should I turn out the light?"—to be answered not by any of us lying snugly in our beds but by a thunderous "Whoo Whoo Whoo" of a very agitated hippo in the river below, clearly distressed by our disturbing light. Needless to say, the light went out to gales of laughter all around.

We fished and hunted as a family. One day we were all creeping along a path intent on finding the big one, my mother bringing up the rear. Suddenly a huge commotion erupted, with noise and snorting and squeals to alert the entire valley! My father, to his regret before knowing what had actually happened, asked if Mom had fallen over. As it happened, a family of warthogs had kept their silence as we walked between them for as long as they could and had erupted in a state of panic, fleeing in every direction! Poor mother's bush craft, as if it was her fault the warthogs had panicked, was continually questioned after that. As to her reaction to my father's blasé comment I know not what.

Incidents at camp were numerous—once an unfortunate hornbill chose to express his total resentment at our presence for hours on end from his perch just above the campfire. Not able to take the days of verbal aggression from the infernal bird, my brother decided to dispatch him to hornbill heaven. Alas, the poor bird had the last laugh, as in his dying throes he clasped the branch below and swiveled downwards with his beady eye fixed on my brother. My advice to anyone is when you see a hornbill, wave, say Hi, and walk away. That damned eye looked at us for a week or more.

A Short Story of Self Discovery in an Age of Innocence

In an attempt to fish one day, I edged out from the bank with my rod onto one the many tree trunks that had succumbed to the rising waters and had tumbled into the river. Imagine in your mind's eye a young lad perched over the flowing water about seven to eight feet from the safety of the bank—hah! Here I was going to catch that giant fighting tiger fish of my dreams, and who had naturally chosen my tree trunk shelter as its home? Things went well for a while—but not one nibble on my offered silver spoon. However, I was not deterred. Suddenly a spasm of pain hit my knee! I looked down to see my legs being invaded by an army of huge black ants headed north! Writhing in agony with ants up my pants, I relinquished the fishing pole to the waters below and headed yelling up the bank. No sympathy from the family, who were more concerned about the missing fishing pole than my private welts!

The most marvelous thing to me was the ability as a preteen to shoulder a .22 and head off alone. Imagine! I would wander off along the game paths and bear witness to Africa in its purest form. I cannot imagine how I was not accosted by the more aggressive predators—how was it that no harm ever came to me? Blissfully unaware, I was able to see the elephants, the magnificent sable antelope, benign crocodiles, wild dogs, and lions—all going about their daily pursuit of survival. What a life I had. You know—maybe I was just too skinny for them to bother.

DAD

A tall man. I saw him from the earliest usually clothed in military uniform, which made his size and appearance doubly impressive to me. He flitted in and out of my life and I usually saw him at breakfast—then again at breakfast the following day! He was firstly an adventurer who loved the thrill of the big-game hunt, then a medical doctor who devoted his time to that pursuit as the generator of funds, and then a military man, in that order.

He had survived World War II. Serving in the 7/9th Royal Scots, he had been wounded and evacuated back to Scotland. After a patch-up, he was dispatched again into combat and in charge of a small detail, only a few hundred men I believe, that were attached to a Canadian Brigade making an invasion attempt into Holland. The Dutch citizenry had breached the polders (dykes) holding back the sea to thwart the German defenses and had swamped the approaches to the town of Middleburg.

The town was host to a Nazi General Daser and several thousand heavily armed "White Bread" troops (so named as they got superior rations based on their military prowess). The only approach to the town was by ungainly and soft-skinned (i.e., not armored) buffalo amphibious troop transports.

Dad led his small band in with no resistance—the Nazis anticipating a huge surge of troops and highly armored tanks! He sent an emissary to demand the general's surrender—the reply came back that the general would not surrender to an officer of lower rank than a colonel (not knowing the laughable troop ratio bluff!).

What to do? In an entirely modest act of self-promotion, my father, a mere major at the time, proceeded to elevate himself in the field! As an "acting" colonel, he went into the town square and accepted the general's surrender. His tiny, nervous band of "jocks" then went about collecting the weapons from the Germans. Faced with approaching nightfall and in an attempt to keep up the charade, my father ordered that the innocent and total harmless buffaloes roar around the streets out of sight of the milling enemy as an illusion of a huge tank movement! The ruse worked, and the morning brought relief. Freedom had come to the city of Middleburg, Holland, as it was finally liberated from the cruel yoke of Nazi Germany. Dad was one of only two or three recipients of the "Dutch Order of the Bronze Lion (Military)"—the highest award given in services rendered their country by the Dutch to foreign servicemen in that brutal occupation. Dad had to go back to being major again…

But at heart he quested for the thrill of the big-game hunt, which was why we ended up in prime safari territory in Africa. Naturally all his sons were taught at a very early age to handle firearms. He had an impressive collection—three of the finest English-made purest Rigbys, various shotguns over the years, and the usual .22s and air guns which we honed in on the range built in the backyard. It was my seventh heaven when invited to help Dad in the ritual cleaning of the rifles. A kettle boiled, hot water poured down the barrels to expand the rifling, then the brass rod, followed by the soothing milky application of oils to maintain absolute, rust-free, total perfection. This was a ritual so solemn as if life depended on it. At first I could not even shoulder the .416—a short, stubby beast no higher than me, intended for elephant and buffalo. But I got to clean it! Ready for action!

This was about as close as I could get to Dad. He would not say much, but in those moments I learned a great deal. He stressed a lot about the discipline of the fire, the hunt. Squeeze the trigger, don't jerk it! Sense the wind, feel it caress your skin—your success depended on it. Look at the signs, the broken twig, footprints in the sand. In his way he was imparting wisdom on all facts of life, except I did not see it until much later. With a rifle cradled, I knew I could crack a one-inch circle by six in the target at one hundred–plus yards—but what I really wanted was just a hug!

He was of course, despite all, my hero. I remember the Dress nights when he would get all prepared, Masta having been pressing and shining, polishing, for days by now—and Dad would emerge in all his finery! Talk about spit and polish! Was I proud—military ribbons and medals jangling and regimental sword at his side—what a scene of perfection for me! I would be up at the Rock the next day challenging and vanquishing all manner of infidels around me.

Thanks, Dad—you didn't say much, but you sure as hell left an impression on a very callow youth, who did not have the maturity at the time to see just where you were trying to get me to see.

MOM

She was a beautiful lass from the Scottish Highlands—tough as nails and hardened by the severe winters and times of deprivation. She bore three sons for my father and doted on them in her own way but never lost sight that her devotion was to him alone, to the day she left this mortal universe. I had a strange relationship with Mom—at times she could be as loving and as giving as a person could be—but then again one could never deny the basic fact that she was for him alone, and this overshadowed all other aspects of her being.

Let's face it—she had an early life not to be envied. She was born in the far north of Scotland—her father the local doctor of the small community of Ullapool, perched on the shores of Loch Broom, a sliver of the sea reaching up into the sparse, heather-covered hills. Buffeted by the unceasing winds of the Atlantic, this was a hard and austere land. All of his patients were poor—they often were only able to pay in kind—a brace of pheasant here, some salmon there—when it could be found. He never failed to hook up the horse and carriage in the depth of winter to head out to the hills to deliver a child, look after an injured crofter, or deliver a sheep (a Scottish one, we only stole English one's, so that's fine)—we are all God's children, after all. That was just how it was. From this humble and remote village, my grandfather elevated himself to the distinguished position of the grand chaplain of the Masonic Grand Lodge of Scotland, located far away in the distant and mighty urban Edinburgh—that in itself is proof to me of how elemental and tough they were.

It was a hard-scrabble existence and survival. Then came the First World War and then on came the Second one. This coming conflagration, caused only, again, by a nation's blind adherence to and promise of a quick-fix salvation by a bankrupt ideology, was poised to send despair around the world. It dispensed its misery on Mom and to her family just a little more than most.

She had her sister go down, gasping for air—torpedoed by a Nazi submarine. She was working as a nurse in a clearly marked hospital ship evacuating children. The direct hit sent those youngsters, panic-stricken, into the cold, frigid waters of the North Atlantic. Big Red Cross on the side of the ship you didn't see—you smirking Nazis! In the early days of the Battle of Britain, her beloved, favorite brother, Johnny, went—just a young lad answering his country's call as a Spitfire pilot, spiraling down in flames. Then poor Alan, captured early on and sent to several POW camps over the five or so long years—he returned alive, but how do we expect anyone's mind to survive that deprivation and hardship? Mom never bought German cars—wonder why?

She excelled at school and sports and had a brilliant and analytic brain. Short of family funds, she managed to follow her calling and became a registered nurse. In a perfect world, she would have been one of the finest medical doctors—witnessed much later by her years of prenatal care and canny highland instinct dispensed to the future mothers of Africa. She met Dad, who was a med student; he drove a superb convertible MG sports car and was accompanied by a black lab—it was love at first sight!

Then the dark curtains of war dropped down for her, and she saw her love abandon his university medical studies and enlist to protect his family and freedom from the invading Hun. The blackout curtains must have had a few pinpricks of light, as they managed, despite the infrequent leave from the military and a serious shrapnel wound on Dad's chest, to concentrate on the delicate and sensual production of two sons! Yes!

I often wonder how she thought about her love when years later she was being propelled across Africa by two Garrett steam locomotives, belching steam and flying cinders of ash over the hot and dusty Kalahari Desert to the promised land of Rhodesia. Good grief, she must have truly, truly loved my father. Three sons to boot—I am sure I did nothing more than whine and complain for food; fortunately I do not remember anything of this at two years of age.

My awakening with my mother was slow as I recall—she was in charge of my comfort, food, and clothing. Most of that became quickly relegated to good old Masta—he had me under control—while she turned her attention back as always to Dad. I don't resent that, but it was a reality. Her day was programmed entirely around him. Let me think—maybe that's the way it is supposed to be?

I did have glimpses inside their devotion, however, as they would invariably sit down in the evenings when he had come back from work. Where they sat depended on the season: either outside, to witness another magnificent African sunset, or in the dry chill of winter, in front of a wood-burning fire.

This would be the platform for the nightly ritual of the glass of brandy and ginger ale. As they sipped it slowly it became the foundation for the discussion of the day's events. I would sidle in and listen to the to and fro. Most of the discussion I did not understand, but it was a warm feeling to be part of the grand design. Moreover, I was privileged to see total love between two beings, and that is a rare thing—matched only, in my experience, by my two quivering and hesitant steenboks that lived over the wall.

On some days Dad would read me a chapter or so of some African hunting classic like *Jock of the Bushveld*! Such bliss—it was fuel to my imagination for the next day to vanquish all that lay before me up at the Rock. More than that, it allowed me a moment of togetherness with my parents that came infrequently, still cherished in memory to this day.

MY BROTHERS

They were away at boarding school for most of my formative years, and I had little interaction with them. Both excelled at sports and thus spent most of their vacation time on the road touring, spending little time at the family home.

As infrequent visitors, they shared a bedroom. I was fortunate to have my own. Excited by their return one week, I remember pestering both of them into playing various games when all they wanted to do was collapse into much-needed catch-up sleep. One day they devised a plan to ensure peace! We were all to embark on a time-trial bike race, over an extensive course of a few miles—and of course I was to be given the honor of starting the first circuit! Little did I realize that it was just a fiendish plot to get some precious and needed sleep! Panting and proud of my time, I arrived back at the house to find them both snoring contentedly! Such is the life of a much younger sibling...

One time they lost a tennis ball upon the roof of the house. The ball was only reachable by climbing up one tree that was conveniently close to the house. As Niall had hoisted it up there in the first place, he was first up the tree—only to come flying down having been stung by those vicious little red wasps! Doug (always the smartie!) decided to use high technology to destroy the wasp nest. He proceeded to get the hosepipe and on full pressure took aim at the nest. Unfortunately for Doug, two high-speed attack wasps followed the stream to its source and zapped him on the nose and cheek, puffing up his eye almost shut! Needless to say, junior here was rolling around in laughter, which did not add to their ill humor...Not to be outfoxed, Doug ran to the gun cabinet and dispatched the nest with the .410 shotgun blast, and both retired to lick their wounds. I still chortle to this day!

From time to time we would meet up on safari, but because of the age difference, I usually did not accompany them on the hunts. We did spend time fishing together, but for the most part I did not know them in those early years.

THE FIFTIES DRIVE-IN

It was a totally, utterly decadent diversion that was loved by all the family! Imagine in your mind's eye a world that had no personal PCs, no mobile phones, none of the modern electronic devices that govern our lives today. There was not even television! That left us with only the big screen—a huge outdoor set of luminous panels reaching up into the sky—surrounded by a semicircle of humped rows and parking bays, divided by the speaker poles. Up on the panels, the projector would send the images of film in living black and white, or as a special treat, Technicolor! This is what we did in Africa to see the idols of the silver screen strut their stuff.

It was a rare event, but when my parents judged a film was of correct-enough morality to be viewed by all the family, the decision was made! Excitement would build and imagination would run riot! Mother would haul out the picnic suitcase—an ingenious hamper of plates, implements, and mugs that would be a sure sign of a feast to come. Here she was able to show her (only?) true culinary wizardry. Just the appearance of the hamper was enough to make my mouth water.

The day would arrive, and in the early evening we would pile into the car—at that time British made Fords I recall, and off we would go in the hope and prayer that the workers in Leyland, England, would not let us down that particular night. Into the arena we would go, speeding over the outlying humps to get to a favorite chosen spot to view the coming scenes. It was an art form: close to the projector building, but not that close to let its light disturb our view. Check the audio—did it work? Yes, volume fine. Ah—near bliss as we settled in with the fading light to watch the forthcoming attractions—or, in my case, got sent off by my parents to burn steam in the playground behind the projector room. Heaven forbid another car would pull up next to us—negative waves and barely concealed hostile stares would emanate from our car, hoping to send the intruders off to another hump.

Darkness almost complete and I would scurry back to the car to settle in to what Hollywood had to offer—to think that today, a mere push of a remote control has replaced this totally and exciting ritual of immersion of the occasion. Soon enough the spool of the huge projectors would signal half time so as to set up the next run. For me, this was the most highly exciting time of the entire night!

For it was now when Mom would venture to the trunk and bring back the hamper. On opening its lid, the most wonderful aroma would fill the car. She had perfected her most cherished recipe—baps with bacon and fried egg. While this might sound very basic but the baps (round, freshly baked, and floury bread rolls) would enclose their suitably warm and delectable filling. Mother had devised a way of keeping the baps warm in this pre-foil age—she wrapped them in a dish cloth and then filled a hot water bottle, which was placed tenderly over the rolls, keeping them steamed right up until intermission. Voila! The most exquisite moment was when you actually burst the yolk—the explosion of yellow would undoubtedly run, dribbling, down your chin. Catch it and devour it. The fast food of today is a mere shadow of such perfection.

Too soon the projectors would spring into life to resume the drama of the day. For me, the drama was over. Replete, I would try to focus on the shimmering images on the screen ahead but usually to no avail. I would succumb like a little puppy and with heavy eyelids drift away in a very rare moment of contentment and thankfulness.

GRANDPARENTS

I was too young really to know them and I remember only snatches of memory from here and there as they flitted into and, equally quickly, out of my life. The first grainy memory is of my Dad's parents, but the most dynamic and forceful persona was Granny Wallace—coming out from the Highlands of Scotland to spend her last days in the bosom of her remaining family.

Her husband had long passed, and I alas never knew him—he was far more than just a local village doctor, I am told. He was also the founder of the local Masonic Lodge and an officer of the Grand Lodge of Scotland. He also had a very firm belief in the positive, anti-carcinogenic powers of greens—broccoli, Brussels sprouts, and the like. He maintained that they had the power to ward off the dreaded cancers that plague us today. How can a man in the remote and cold north of Scotland have such insight? Journals of medicine to this day offer many various theses of the preventative power of the simple cabbage. Amazing.

To me his greatest legacy was his fundamental belief in and adherence to the idea that a "wee dram" of the finest Scotch whiskey taken religiously each night was the finest and most restorative tonic known to man. My parents stuck to that teaching with fervor close to that matching a cult's. However, living in Africa, they changed the brew to the more locally available brandy. I suspect he would have forgiven them, as the message remained intact. This very same message has continued downwards along the line—pesky things, genes, aren't they? My brothers and I, not willing to risk angering the old man and our health, follow his prescription to this day. Maybe and only on rare occasions we might stray into two wee drams—don't want risk ill health and to tempt fate, you understand! In tough times I suspect that all three of us draw on that long-forgotten but inherent strength he dispensed to us.

Into my life came his wife, Granny Wallace—a formidable woman who scared me to death. She was not happy to be in Africa and missed her beloved home on the shores of Loch Broom, Ullapool. For years after the death of the doctor, she had operated a very successful shop selling local handicrafts—the forerunner of today's efforts to give growth and life to those on the edge of poverty in the most rural and remote glens of the Scottish north. Yet here she was in the heat of Africa, gasping like a fish out of water. She did not have too much time for me and could see right through my whining and complaining. Although—when nobody was looking and sensing her mortality, she would take me into her arms and envelope me in her huge bosom and give me a bone-crushing and lovingly memorable hug! God—what an experience! Where the hell did that come from? Soon that damn big "C" came to claim her, and she was gone.

My other Granny, Granny J, was a totally different number. Grandfather (note, no shortening here) on my Dad's side was tall and silent and sent me into a state of total panic and dumb stupefaction. He neither volunteered nor returned conversation easily. Also a successful medical doctor, he had come out to Africa to retire. He had a habit of smoking pipes and filling his living room with the most gorgeous aromas of tobacco, maple, and rum. I would sit at his feet and inhale these wonderful aromas—scant regard or cognizance of secondhand smoke in those days!

Years later when we had inherited his pipe cabinet, I would fill one of his pipes and imagine I was the old man, puffing away and dispensing sage advice. With much hemming and hawing, I told my imaginary, fawning and ever-attentive audiences about their health as I puffed vigorously away at the pipe. Many more years later, I filled the pipes with tobacco and lit the things—it did not take long after violent fits of coughing and wheezing I realized it was an art form I could learn later if absolutely necessary. Alas the genetic failure that followed Grandfather's line, sadly even to this day, coupled with the daily intake of tobacco, led to the hardening of his arteries. I remember Dad having his aircraft metal technicians fabricate a static bicycle for Grandfather to exercise his remaining leg—a simple device far ahead of today's fitness machines. Sadly it was way too late to solve the accumulation of the sedentary habits of a lifetime.

His wife Granny J—she was a hoot. I loved to go visit her—they lived in town not far away and close to the city park. She was on a very different plane from her husband—almost I think even a little distracted, if not to put too fine a point on it. She never had any trouble delivering a hug! She would walk me down to the park and put me on the swings and roundabouts and giggle with joy as I whirled around! To me she was a real person, not far from a child herself and who had little time for the stiff formalities of life—after all, a tad of insanity does us all good! To her the playground was a momentary escape from years of suppressed emotions and a life so far from her rustic roots. (Lordy—did any of this flow down to moi?)

She knew that all a young lad wanted was a smile and to be spoiled by hugs and attention—with loads of food at all times. No manners needed here—what a luxury when faced with all those rules of dos and don'ts.

HATFIELD PRIMARY SCHOOL

Thank God I had the Rock. It was my escape after hours of purgatory during all my years spent at the local school. I had no enthusiasm for school I was taking in the glory and pleasures of a barefooted life of freedom—wandering along the paths of my natural world across the wall, exploring in wonderment of the seasons and the discovery of all that Africa could give to me. Then like a sledgehammer coming down right between my eyebrows was—school!

After a few desultory pick-ups and drop-offs, it was decided I could just as easily bike my way. To me it was not a problem as I loved the downhill—the pleasant softness of the early morning wind across my cheeks would lull me into a state of submission of what was to come.

You know about the semi-curdled milk. The next memory was the polio vaccination! Of standing in the hot sun in a line waiting for a barbaric invasion of one's arm. The authorities were not content with that, a few years later we had to repeat the performance with a sugar cube—these exercises have tainted my trust in government to this day.

Life at the school then was, for me, immense boredom, faced with mediocre teachers with even less enthusiasm. I did love sports however and took every available opportunity to play whatever game the season offered. I think I even elected basket weaving at some stage as it was held outside of the classroom under the trees, thank you! The course was given by a blonde goddess that captivated me—I know I never really made a very good basket ever, actually.

Johnny was my closest and only friend at school. Then one day, to my intense confusion and bewilderment, he came up to me, accompanied by his much larger brother and friends, and told me that I had in some way deserved a fight. What? The bigger boys arranged a rough circle around us—I am sure Johnny did not want this as much as I. Into combat we went—he rushed me and I tripped him. This was immediately judged a foul by his brother—why, I ask? But no one was listening to me—the power of the mob had taken control! So back it was to the arena—two seven-year-old gladiators circling each other with absolutely no intent of hurting one another and both frantically wondering, "How the hell do I get out of this?" So we both went at it until Johnny senior decided that enough was enough and we were both led off. The last laugh was on Johnny senior, because from that day on, his brother and I became the closest of friends.

It was another huge pedal uphill to Johnny's place, much sharper than the one back home—no wonder I remained a skinny wretch. All that cycling. It did have its rewards in that at our annual Sports Day, they actually awarded the person who could stand in place on a bicycle without falling over for the longest time. Guess who—me?! Anyway, Johnny was the son of Greek immigrants, and I loved the immersion into his life that he allowed me—his mother welcomed me as just another son. Towards the end of our life at the primary school, she gave Johnny a birthday party to which all the class was invited.

Such excitement! Remember, up until now I had limited interaction with other kids except for the few hours of schooling, and then I would flee up to my isolation and consolation at the Rock. Here I was being invited to a party! I asked Johnny if girls were going to be there. "Of course,"

A Short Story of Self Discovery in an Age of Innocence

he said—he was, I suspect, years ahead of me in my isolationist stricture. "Oh," I said, meekly but with heart pounding. This was to be my first exposure to the other side, and I was mortified.

So the night came—I pedaled down the hill and up the hill, wondering about this event and conjuring up wild ideas as only an eleven-year-old can do. Johnny, of course, had invited the entire class—no problem to him, being such a cosmopolitan dude. His mom was there and God bless her soul, she looked over us with just as much rein as she deemed fit. As a Greek mom, she never let things get out of hand. What she did not know was that Johnny had set up a game out back where the boys would sneak in to get a kiss from the girls, only if they said the right things. My turn came, and I convinced my worth to Manuela from Mozambique! It was winter, and her lips were kinda rough and chapped—not enough to deter me, however.

I fled down the hill and up the long hill to home—no thought given to the pedals flying around and around. I was awake to the other side! Hallelujah!

A DEFINING MOMENT

We were in the Zambezi River Valley—hot, dry, and rugged. The escarpment hills rose up just a few miles on either side of the mighty flow of water, which had cut through for millions of years. It had forced through a volcanic fault line of hard-scrabble basalt rock and had resulted in a series of ravines. Little rain fell here. It was a parched, sterile environment that gave no quarter and did not expect much in return.

It was here that I set off on my first elephant hunt! Of course, it was only in my mind really—armed with my big-game rifle, I was out to conquer the biggest bull of them all. Dad had allowed me to come along, and I was given my beloved .22 gauge so as to be part of the action! The African elephant is bestowed by nature with huge tusks over its Asian relative and thus sadly the given totem of the biggest hunting prize. Anyway—my father and I took off with the professional hunter in the Land Rover in search of the ivory tusks that would ultimately hang not as intended on a living triumph of God's creation, but on an egoistic wall of human "achievement." I was seated on the middle seat of the Land Rover, not sure what I had to do but sure feeling included and ready to go. No thought was given to the gas tank I was sitting on (remember—the marvel of British engineering) as the temperature climbed to well over 130 degrees.

We set off and reached the flat plain beyond the escarpment and traveled along a narrow rut for a few miles. After no sign of life, a decision was made to head back the river, which entailed winding along the ever-rougher track up a series of slight hills before it dropped suddenly into the jumbled ravines of the escarpment. Suddenly, on the crest, we stopped! Lurching out of my dreamland of mighty trophies that I was about to claim, I focused on the way ahead. Dust! Behind the haze, swirling mirages unfolded a scurrying herd of vast, grey creatures. I had no idea what I was seeing. Dad and the hunter knew immediately—it was elephants, and the hunt was on!

Grabbing their stubby but immensely lethal rifles, they left the vehicle, testing the wind and determining that a circuitous route would keep the herd oblivious. They would then be able to see if any big bulls were about. A hushed voice from Dad told me, "Stay in the Land Rover. Don't move; you will be OK." Besides, I thought to myself, I have the .22—powerful enough to save me from the worst! So off they went. I was mesmerized, stuck in the Land Rover—watching all unfold in ghastly slow definition in front of me, paralyzed in fear.

Circling around, keeping the wind to their advantage, the two hunters crept. They were seeking out a bull. Alas, it was a breeding herd. Suddenly a huge noise and trumpeting came out of nowhere—a pregnant elephant that had been left behind by the herd to be alone in her labor and to minimize danger had picked up the downwind scent of my dad! All antennas raised, she passed right in front of me and was headed directly towards Dad at an ever-increasing pace. She was determined to take out this threat to her and her unborn and reunite into the safety of the herd.

I was petrified. It seemed to be all happening in slow motion—watching my dad and the hunter yelling, waving their hats, trying desperately to give this poor mum advance warning to steer away from them. I tried screaming a warning, but no sound escaped my lips. Not to be deterred, she picked up pace and advanced with strident bellows, ears erect and trunk aloft, screaming towards her perceived threat. I cringed further and further into my seat as I saw my father about to be met head on...

The first shot rang out—followed by, what seemed to me, a repetition of bangs, bangs, bangs...

It was a moment of pure terror. I did not know what to do. I imagined my father being impaled by the very ivory tusks he so sought after! A silence... I looked up and saw this magnificent beast stopped in its tracks, and then- as if in a salute to the ultimate aggressor—raise her trunk and give a final hurrah to those who had mown her down. The rear legs went down first, then collapsing slowly, she turned on her side and exhaled for the last time, her huge pregnant belly exposed to the rude, harsh, dry sun of the Zambezi Valley.

This was the day I gave up the rifle and passed into manhood.

* * *

Printed in Great Britain
by Amazon.co.uk, Ltd.,
Marston Gate.